T0142435

GOD'S BAPTISM *with* *the* HOLY SPIRIT

SAMUEL SIDERS

authorHOUSE®

AuthorHouse™
1663 Liberty Drive
Bloomington, IN 47403
www.authorhouse.com
Phone: 1 (800) 839-8640

Published by AuthorHouse 01/17/2018

ISBN: 978-1-5462-2336-8 (sc)
ISBN: 978-1-5462-2335-1 (e)

Library of Congress Control Number: 2018900084

Print information available on the last page.

PREFACE

The content of this book will be providing the answer for these questions: How is the Baptism WITH the Holy Spirit different from God's New Birth, Water baptism, and God's multiple anointing for ministry? What is the Baptism WITH the Holy Spirit as recorded in John chapters 14-16, Acts chapters 1-2, and 1 Corinthians chapters 12-14? Is this Baptism for us today? How do we receive this Baptism? What is God's purpose for this Baptism?

There are many who falsely believe the Nine Gifts of the Holy Spirit (charismata) ended in the First Century AD. Over the years as an Apologist I have had to research to find HISTORICAL information which proves that conclusion is false. As a result, I found HISTORICAL information that substantiates that the "charismata" has never ceased to be manifested by God throughout the centuries. This Book contains that HISTORICAL information.

This book is also to share the overwhelming benefits God has included with the Glossolalia and Power of God that the Baptism with His Holy Spirit provides for us to be more victorious in our obedience to Him, more than conquerors as a Greater threat to Satan and the kingdom of Darkness, and to DEFEND God's Holy Spirit Baptism by using History and the Scriptures relevant to this subject. It has been Satan's agenda to deceive against the Baptism with the Holy Spirit because of the THREAT God's Baptism makes us against Satan's wicked agenda which is to keep us weak and anemic, and to discourage those who profess to be Born Again Christians from ever receiving this GOD GIVEN Baptism by deceiving Preachers to disparage and blaspheme God's Baptism WITH the Holy Spirit.

Your Brother and follow servant of Jesus Christ
Samuel R. Siders

CONTENTS

CHAPTER ONE

GOD'S NEW BIRTH

The cause of God's New Birth Life Changing Event (2 Corinthians 5:17) is when the Holy Spirit removes the "sinful nature" from our spirit/soul and replaces it with God's "Righteous Nature," and according to 1 John 3:9 our spirit cannot sin any more as long as God's righteous nature (seed) remains in our spirit. This means that our spirit/soul cannot sin, and that our spirit/soul obeys God's Ethical Laws 24/7 (Jeremiah 31:33, Ezekiel 36:26). Jeremiah 31:33 and Ezekiel 36:26 define what happens when we are born again by God's Spirit. A righteous nature cannot sin or it would not be a righteous nature.

God's New Birth radically and instantaneously transforms our spirit and soul from sinner to saint. Apostle Paul in Romans 7:22-25 lets us know that a sinful nature remains in our physical body (flesh) and it is because of this fact that the sinful nature in our physical body will constantly "war" against the righteous nature of God in our spirit in the attempt to take control of how we live our life while in our PHYSICAL BODY, and a proof that God … never … removes our FREE WILL choice to obey God's righteous nature in our spirit or the sinful nature in our physical body. The topic about "works" AFTER receiving Jesus' Atonement and God's New Birth is not intended to be fully explained in this book, although some comments will be included.

It is a fact that because of the New Birth we will obey God's Ethical Laws as a result of this Event, but "free will" and the "temptations of the sinful nature" in our physical body (flesh) will be the hindrance to our perfectly obeying God's Ethical Laws, like our spirit and soul does and compels us to do (1 John 3:9). Jesus and the Apostles WARN us against allowing the sinful nature in our physical body to control our life, and there is plenty of Scripture to explain how serious it is if we do not make the CONSCIOUS EFFORT to resist the sinful nature; as Paul wrote "die daily," "living sacrifice," and Jesus said "pick up your cross and follow me." Aside from Jesus explaining the need to be born again to enter the Kingdom of God, Apostle Paul wrote in Romans 8:5 if we are not born again by God's Spirit we … are not … His.

There are many in churches today who foolishly believe Religious Ritualistic Observance, going through the motions of "Christianity," provides eternal life, never having received God's New Birth. BIBLICAL Christianity is not a religion, "ritualistic observance;" it is a RELATIONSHIP and FELLOWSHIP (Revelation 3:20) with the God who created ALL things that HE has provided through Jesus' atonement and the New Birth. Many Religious people will end up in the Lake of Fire because they have … never … been Born Again by God's Spirit. It is because of God's New Birth in our "spirit and soul" that "sanctification" is perfect and complete (1 John 3:9), but in our "physical body" since a sinful nature remains, "sanctification" is a gradual lifelong progressive process that requires our "free will choice" for this to occur.

God will not force us to obey Him, live holy lives, we must … choose … to obey Him and He has provided the "power" through the Baptism WITH the Holy Spirit to make it possible so we can. Paul confirms the differences as written in Philippians 3:11-16. Jesus' righteousness through His Blood Atonement makes us righteous in our spirit and soul, but not in our physical body; it is for this reason God will use the temptations of the sinful nature in our physical body and suffering (chastening) to present our physical body blameless, undefiled, without spot or wrinkle at the Second Coming of Jesus so that the immortal body that we have "hoped" to receive will be given to us (Romans 8:23-25, 1 Corinthians 15:53-54, 1 John 3:2-3).

God's Plan of Salvation does not only encompass our spirit and soul, but also our physical body and it is for this reason our physical body undergoes a lifelong progressive sanctification process. Jesus let us know that BOTH the soul and body of those who reject Him will be in the lake of fire, not the soul only (Matthew 10:28). Apostle Paul as a result of his prayer in 1 Thessalonians 5:23 affirms our spirit, soul, AND BODY are intended by God to be blameless, not having spot or wrinkle, but holy and without blemish (Ephesians 5:27). Jesus let us know in Revelation 3:1-5 if we RESIST the process, which is going onto perfection in our physical body, our name COULD be removed from the book of life.

There is plenty of Scripture to support God will hold us accountable for the sin we commit with our physical body, that … COULD … have eternal negative consequences, and why Paul also taught we must "mortify (put to death) the desires of the flesh;" RESIST the sinful desires of our physical body, to obey the righteous nature of God that is in our spirit and soul. One of the many wonderful provisions included in Jesus' Atonement, is that GOD FOREKNEW we would struggle to Perfectly obey Him, His Standard of Holiness; therefore He has provided for us to be forgiven of our occasional failure as long as we ARE making the … CONSCIOUS EFFORT… to improve in our obedience; conform to His expectations of us. Two proof texts written to those of us who are born again by God's Spirit for forgiveness are 2 Peter 3:9 and 1 John 2:1.

The Lord is not slack concerning his promise, as some men count slackness; but is longsuffering TOWARD US, not willing that any should perish, but that all should come to repentance. 2 Peter 3:9

My little children, these things write I unto you, THAT YOU SIN NOT. And if any man sin, we have an advocate with the Father, Jesus Christ the righteous: 1 John 2:1

Jesus had to Die AND Resurrect, for God's New Birth to be given to us, and the promise under the New Covenant to be complete; not only to provide God's Blood Atonement for our sin to be forgiven and cleansed but also to provide the New Birth we receive under the New Covenant (Isaiah 53:10-12, Jeremiah 31:31-34). If a person is not Born Again (anagenneo) by God's Spirit FIRST, water baptism has no value. It is an error to conclude that the "Fruit of the Spirit" (holiness) is proof of a Christian having the Acts 2:2-4 Baptism WITH the Holy Spirit. The "Fruit of the Spirit" (holiness) is the manifested proof a person is Truly BORN AGAIN by God's Spirit; God's extravagant Love being among the most prominent.

Therefore if any man be in Christ, he is a new creature: old things are passed away; behold all things are become new. 2 Corinthians 5:17

Whosoever is born of God does not commit sin; for his seed remains in him: and he cannot sin, because he is born of God. 1 John 3:9

But this shall be the covenant that I will make with the house of Israel; After those days, says the Lord, I will put my law in their inward parts, and write it in their hearts; and will be their God, and they shall be my people. Jeremiah 31:33

A new heart also will I give you, and a new spirit will I put within you: and I will take away the stony heart out of your flesh, and I will give you a heart of flesh. Ezekiel 36:26

For I delight in the law of God after the inward man: But I see another law in my members,

warring against the law of my mind, and bringing me into captivity to the law of sin which is in my members. O wretched man that I am! Who shall deliver me from the body of this death? I thank God through Jesus Christ our Lord. So then with the mind I serve the law of God; but with the flesh the law of sin. Romans 7:22-25

God's Power given through the Baptism with the Holy Spirit gives us a greater potential to resist the sinful desires of the physical body (flesh), and we are held accountable if we do not resist (Romans 8:1-14, 2 Corinthians 5:9-10, Revelation 3:2-5, Revelation 22:12). With God's Power there is no excuse for committing sin, but a Free Will CHOICE we have made not to resist the temptation to sin. God's "Righteous Nature" contains the "Fruit of the Spirit," HIS Moral Character. Paul wrote in Galatians 5:22-24 what the "Fruit of God's Spirit" is, and John in 1 John 2:9, 2:11, 3:15, and 4:20 clarifies if we hate (which would include holding a grudge instead of immediately forgiving) it is proof a person is still in darkness (not born again). Those who are TRULY Born Again by God's Spirit, hate no one, hold no grudges, and forgive without having to be asked; if this is otherwise true about you, you need to reexamine yourself to discern if you are truly one of God's people (born again).

There is therefore now no condemnation to them which are in Christ Jesus, who walk not after the flesh, but after the Spirit ...Therefore, brethren, we are debtors, not to the flesh, to live after the flesh. For if you live after the flesh, you shall die: but if you through the Spirit do mortify the deeds of the body, you shall live. For as many as are led by the Spirit of God, they are the sons of God. Romans 8:1-14

Wherefore we labor, that, whether present or absent, we may be accepted of him. For we must all appear before the Judgment Seat of Christ; that every one may receive the things done in his body, according to that he has done, whether it be good or bad. 2 Corinthians 5:9-10

And, behold, I come quickly; and my reward (Gr. reward and punishment) is with me, to give every man according as his work shall be. Revelation 22:12

Be watchful, and strengthen the things which remain, that are ready to die: for I have not found your works perfect before God. Remember therefore how you have received and heard, and hold fast, and repent. If therefore you shall not watch, I will come on you as a thief, and you shall not know what hour I will come upon you. You have a few names even in Sardis which have not defiled their garments; and they shall walk with me in white: for they are worthy. He that overcomes, the same shall be clothed in white raiment; and I will not blot out his name out of the book of life, but I will confess his name before my Father, and before his angels. Revelation 3:2-5

But the fruit of the Spirit is love, joy, peace, longsuffering, gentleness, goodness, faith, Meekness, temperance: against such there is no law. And they that are Christ's have crucified the flesh with the affections and lusts. Galatians 5:22-24

He that says he is in the light, and hates his brother, is in darkness even until now. 1 John 2:9

CHAPTER TWO

WATER BAPTISM

John the Baptist lets us know in Matthew 3:11 that water baptism is FOR a past action of repentance (Strong's #1519), and why John required the Rabbis to have repented before he would baptize them (Matthew 3:8). In John 1:33 John the Baptist tells us that God commissioned him to baptize in water, and explains why in Acts 19:3 his baptism is called "John's Baptism." There was no Mosaic Law for John's form of water baptism until John; therefore he was the first one who God commissioned to do this, and afterwards Jesus taught His first Apostles to continue water baptism, which John 3:22-26 validates, Jesus commanded as written in Mark 16:16, why Peter said to do this in Acts 2:38, and was being done throughout the Book of Acts.

There are those who FALSELY teach Jesus had committed sin during His lifetime, to explain why Jesus had to be baptized in water, like we are commanded to do. There is … nothing … written in the Bible to validate that Jesus ever sinned in His lifetime, but that does not stop them from twisting and perverting Scripture to support their erroneous accusation against Jesus having … never… sinned; therefore Jesus' statement "to fulfill all righteousness" was He being baptized as an EXAMPLE for what we would have to do to complete God's Plan of Salvation to make us "whole" through Him. There are also False Prophets who claiming to be Jesus' Second Coming misuse Scripture to teach Jesus sinned and that He was crucified for this reason; not only for ours but for His also, another TOTALLY false teaching.

A sacrifice for sin must be perfect in every way, Jesus is this perfection. We are born with sinful natures and for this reason we are born sinners. Like Adam was created without any sinful nature so was Jesus in Mary's womb and as a result was born a Saint not a sinner. In Luke 1:35 the Greek translated "holy one" should be translated "holy saint." It is through God's New Birth we are transformed from sinner to saint, and why it is a fallacy to state "we are all sinners saved by grace." If we are Truly saved by grace (Jesus' Atonement) God no longer calls us sinners,

HE calls us saints; therefore it is God's intent that our lifestyle conforms to what HE calls us, and why as written in Romans 8:28-30 God has predestined (established) that certain events would happen in our life to conform our physical body into the sinless example of His ONLY begotten Son Jesus, but as previously shared our "free will" will determine how rapidly this process of physical body sanctification will occur.

There are an overwhelming amount of false accusations being laid against Jesus contrary to the Scriptures and the veracity of the Bible in the world today, so many lies and deceptions that it is astonishing. It is Apologists like me who am constantly being made privy to these accusations so that we can Defend Jesus and the Bible against the satanic Lies and Deceptions that unlearned naïve gullible people fall prey to "hook line and sinker." It is written that Jesus was tempted in ALL points as we but without sin," and "though He is the Son learned obedience through the things He suffered" (Hebrews 4:15 and 5:8). These two statements about Jesus must be used to come to a correct understanding of Jesus' life. The "suffering to learn obedience" is the "temptations" Jesus experienced, like all of us do, so He could learn how ... NOT ... to sin; Jesus "aced" ALL these attacks, but clearly we never do.

Water Baptism has a different purpose to complete God's Plan of Salvation for us to be made completely "whole" in body and spirit. When the Greek is used for John 3:25 and 1 Peter 3:21; the purpose is not just an "outward sign of an inward change." Using the Greek definition for the word "purifying" in John 3:25, God uses the ritual of water baptism to Cleanse our soul from the Guilt of sin.

Jesus' Blood Atonement FORGIVES us of the guilt of sin; God uses water baptism to CLEANSE (purify us of) the guilt that sin caused. There is … no … place where the Scriptures teach that the Baptism WITH the Holy Spirit (Power, Glossolalia, and Nine Gifts [charismata]) is Required to receive eternal life, but there is that God's NEW BIRTH … IS … required, which necessitated the NEED for Jesus to resurrect (Romans 4:25, 1 Peter 1:3). Jesus' Blood redeems our soul … not … water baptism (Revelation 1:5 and 5:9).

Using the Greek definition for the words "now saves us" and "good conscience toward God" in 1 Peter 3:21 tells me this verse could have been better translated. The word "saves" misleads a person to believe we are born again through water baptism or that we receive the promise and hope of eternal life through water baptism, and will contribute to misinterpreting John 3:3-6; this is not what the Greek is implying. In this verse the Greek word "sozo" (sode'-zo) would have been better translated "now heals us" or "now restores our soul to health." Sin has damaged and infected our soul to the point that a healing is needed, and God uses the ritual of water baptism like a medicine to accomplish that healing. The other phrase "good conscience toward God," as a result of all that is written here would mean "the answer of a good, cleansed, purified, and healthy spirit/soul toward God."

God uses the blood of Jesus (atonement) to FORGIVE and CLEANSE our sin, and water baptism to CLEANSE the guilt of sin and to HEAL our soul of the damage sin has caused; the depth of this is awesome. For anyone to teach or believe water baptism is an OPTION to ignore they have chosen to be Deceived and Unlearned against WHY Jesus and the Apostles taught we ARE REQUIRED to do this AFTER we repent of our sins to receive Jesus as Lord and Savior of our life. "Repent AND be baptized" has specific and significant reasons for BOTH being required of us that are not to be ignored.

Do YOU want to be made perfectly whole? If it is possible for us to be baptized in water we are do it as soon as possible AFTER we have been born again by God's Spirit. As for those who die before they can be baptized, God's Grace [Jesus' atonement] covers that inability, like the man on the cross who did not have the opportunity or a person who receives Jesus as Lord and Savior on their death bed, extenuating circumstances that prevent them; therefore God will show mercy, like Jesus' reprimand of the Rabbis concerning the Sabbath, "if you had understood what this means that I would have mercy and not judgment you would not have condemned the guiltless."

Chapter Three

God's Baptism with the Holy Spirit

There is a verse that can be used to validate the Baptism WITH the Holy Spirit was never intended to end until Jesus' Second Coming, which is 1 Corinthians 1:7 and needs to be remembered when interpreting 1 Corinthians 13:10; "that which is perfect is COME" is Jesus' Second Coming. There is a lot of history about the Baptism that needs to be shared to create a foundation for what the Bible has to teach about the Baptism with the Holy Spirit, which I have had to research over the years, and much more in the past ten years because of all the foolish and blind conclusions I have been made privy to as an Apologist. One History I had found states the Baptism with the Holy Spirit was COMMON until the persecution ended in the fourth century and did not resume being COMMON until after the Reformation during the Great Holiness Revivals of the eighteenth century (1700s) to this day.

So that you come behind in no gift; waiting for the coming of our Lord Jesus Christ: 1 Corinthians 1:7

But when that which is perfect is come, then that which is in part shall be done away. When I was a child, I spoke as a child; I understood as a child, I thought as a child: but when I became a man, I put away childish things. For now we see through a glass, darkly; but then ... FACE TO FACE ...; now I know in part; but then shall I know even as also I am known. 1 Corinthians 13:10-12

People who are taught that the Baptism ended in the first century are told LIES, and obviously unaware because they have not done their OWN research to the extent ... necessary ... to find out that they have been LIED to. Another LIE is that which the Holy Spirit gives today started around the beginning of the twentieth century; Azusa Street in 1906 Los Angeles California. For William J. Seymour to be a student of a well-known PENTECOASTAL preacher Charles Parham, proves the Baptism with the Holy Spirit was still in existence before William and the Azusa St. revival; amazing a person's choice to be Unlearned and Blind in heart and mind to ignore this. The Baptism WITH the Holy Spirit is as much for us today as the Baptism was in the first century, and every bit as much needed. The only reason the Baptism … appeared … to have ended, is CORRUPTION in the Catholic Church, but I am totally convinced that GOD has always had a "remnant" in EVERY century that had the Baptism with the Holy Spirit, but was not well documented in every century for us to know with certainty.

Here are some other reports I found in my research for the Glossolalia and Nine Gifts being manifested over the centuries that were documented after the first century and before the twentieth century:

[150 C.E. … Justin Martyr wrote "For the prophetical gifts remain with us, even to this present time," and "Now, it is possible to see amongst us women and men who possess gifts of the Spirit of God."]

[156-172 … Montanus and his two prophetesses— Maximilla and Priscilla—spoke in tongues and saw this as evidence of the presence of the Holy Spirit.]

[175 C.E. ... Irenaeus of Lyons, in his treatise Against Heresies, speaks positively of those in the church "who through the Spirit speak all kinds of languages."]

[230 C.E. ... Novatian said, "This is He who places prophets in the Church, instructs teachers, directs tongues, gives powers and healings... and thus make the Lord's Church everywhere, and in all, perfected and completed."]

[340 C.E. ... Hilary of Poitiers, echoing Paul in 1 Corinthians, wrote, "For God hath set same in the Church, first apostles... secondly prophets... thirdly teachers... next mighty works, among which are the healing of diseases... and gifts of either speaking or interpreting diverse kinds of tongues."]

[390 C.E. ... Augustine of Hippo, in an exposition on Psalm 32, discusses a phenomenon contemporary to his time of those who "sing in jubilation," not in their own language, but in a manner that "may not be confined by the limits of syllables."]

[5th century ... St. Patrick of Ireland (c. 387–493); in The Confession of St. Patrick, records hearing a strange language being prayed by the Holy Spirit in a dream. St. Patrick says in his book: "And another night – God knows, I do not, whether within me or beside me – most words which I heard and could not understand, except at the end of the speech it was represented thus: 'He who gave his life for you, he it is who speaks within you.' And thus I awoke, joyful." And on a second occasion I saw Him praying within me, and I was as it were, inside my own body, and I heard Him above me—that is, above my inner self. He was praying powerfully with sighs.

And in the course of this I was astonished and wondering, and I pondered who it could be who was praying within me. But at the end of the prayer it was revealed to me that it was the Spirit. And so I awoke and remembered the Apostle's words: "Likewise the Spirit helps us in our weakness; for we know not how to pray as we ought. But the Spirit Himself intercedes for us with sighs too deep for utterance [Romans 8:26]." And again: "The Lord our advocate intercedes for us (Romans 8:27).]

[500 - 1000 C.E. ... During the so-called Dark Ages, little history was recorded although speaking in tongues may well have been practiced in certain times and places.]

[1100s ... The Waldenses and Albigenses, as well as certain of the orthodox Franciscans, all reportedly spoke in tongues. Saint Hildegard of Bingen is also reputed to have spoken and sung in tongues, and her spiritual songs were referred to by contemporaries as "concerts in the Spirit."]

[1300s ... The Moravians are referred to by detractors as having spoken in tongues. John Roche, a contemporary critic, claimed that the Moravians "commonly broke into some disconnected jargon, which they often passed upon those who reproached, 'as the exuberant and resistless Evacuations of the Spirit.']

[17th century ... The French Prophets: The Camisards also spoke sometimes in languages that were unknown: "Several persons of both Sexes," James Du Bois of Montpellier recalled, "I have heard in their Ecstasies pronounce certain words, which seemed to the Standers-by, to be some Foreign Language." These utterances were sometimes accompanied by the gift of interpretation exercised, in Du Bois' experience, by the same person who had spoken in tongues.]

[1600s ... Early Quakers, such as Edward Burrough, make mention of tongues speaking in their meetings: "We spoke with new tongues, as the Lord gave us utterance, and His Spirit led us."]

[1700s ... John Wesley and Methodism; Wesleyan revivals across Europe and North America included many reportedly miraculous events, including speaking in tongues.]

[1800s ... Edward Irving and the Catholic Apostolic Church; Edward Irving, a minister in the Church of Scotland, wrote of a woman who would "speak at great length, and with superhuman strength, in an unknown tongue, to the great astonishment of all who heard." Irving further stated that "tongues are a great instrument for personal edification, however mysterious it may seem to us."]

[1817 ... In Germany, Gustav von Below, an aristocratic officer of the Prussian Guard, and his brothers, founded a charismatic movement based on their estates in Pomerania, which may have included speaking in tongues.]

Everything I will share is Totally BIBLE supported about the Baptism WITH the Holy Spirit. It has been clear to me for years when people ignore that Jesus and ... ALL ... of the Apostles had this Baptism, when reading Scriptures related to the Holy Spirit, they constantly misuse and misinterpret many Scriptures about Him, His functions, and the purpose that Jesus preached and taught the Apostles for them to teach what they wrote. It is amazing some of the purposeful Blind conclusions those who do not have this Baptism come to about the Holy Spirit when reading the Scriptures. When blasphemers and naysayers speak against the Baptism with the Holy Spirit, they prove two things; they do not have the Baptism with the Holy Spirit and their comprehension is woefully lacking. Reality is, unless a person has the Baptism with the Holy Spirit they will be at a disadvantage to understand everything God has revealed to me, and they should … NEVER … teach anything about the Baptism or speak a negative opinion, to avoid being guilty of blaspheming the Holy Spirit.

The Holy Spirit takes Jesus' place on earth for our benefit as lawyer, intercessor, helper, and teacher; John 14:26 "But the Comforter (Parakletos, masculine noun), which is the Holy Spirit, whom the Father will send in my name, HE shall teach you all things, and bring all things to your remembrance, whatsoever I have said unto you," and in John 14:17 that God's Holy Spirit would dwell in us. Naysayers have a misconception against Jesus being God's Promised Messiah when they read Jeremiah 31:34, to falsely claim Jesus is not HE. Knowing Jeremiah 31:33 defines God's New Birth, and what Jesus taught the Holy Spirit will do in our life, what Jeremiah 31:34 says … ONLY … applies to those who have been Born Again by God's Spirit … not … to those who have not. Not only that ALL from the least to the greatest of those who are born again need no man to teach them, but also because of Jesus' blood Atonement God will not remember our sins anymore; we will be forgiven and cleansed of them.

What Jeremiah 31:34 says does not mean God will not use Apostles, Prophets, Evangelists, Pastors and Teachers (Ephesians 4:12) to improve our knowledge, obedience to God, and understanding of the Scriptures and God's Kingdom; what it does mean is that there are DEEP THINGS, SECRETS, and MYSTERIES of God that GOD has reserved for HIM SELF to teach and reveal to us which no man can. An example of this is what Jesus said in John 6:44-45 "No man can come to me, except the Father which has sent me draw him: and I will raise him up at the last day. It is written in the prophets, And they shall be all taught of God. Every man therefore that has heard, and has learned from the Father, comes unto me." Without the HELP of the Holy Spirit there is information God has for us that we will never learn. Aside from this Fact … no one … will ever be persuaded God exists and they need Jesus to receive eternal life unless God's Spirit proves BOTH to them, like He has done for those of us who are Truly Born Again by God's Spirit.

The Greek word translated Comforter (KJV), parakletos (par-ak'-lay-tos) in John 14:26 and other verses, refers to the Holy Spirit as being our advocate to stand in our defense as a legal aid. The meaning also extends to Him being our securer, to lead us into a deeper knowledge and understanding of the Scriptures, and to give us divine strength against adversity. One of the English words that we get from the Greek prefix "Para" is paralegal who serves as an assistant. Paralegal: of, relating to, or being a paraprofessional who assists a layer. Paraprofessional: a trained aide who assists a professional person (as a teacher or doctor) Para: beside: alongside of: beyond: aside from.

But the Helper (lawyer, advocate, legal counsel), which is the Holy Spirit, whom the Father will send in my name, HE shall teach you all things, and bring all things to your remembrance, whatsoever I have said unto you. John 14:26 (NKJV)

God's Baptism with the Holy Spirit also is given to instruct or teach us what God's perfect will for our life is more perfectly and the Scriptures, and to give us the power to do what He has taught and revealed to us. To show us the way how to please God to the fullest of His expectation for us, as individuals for why we were born, and to be accepted rather than rejected at the Judgment Seat of Christ. With this train of thought I see Jesus as the Parakletos for his disciples, praying and interceding in their behalf while He was on the earth.

When Jesus went back to the Father, the Holy Spirit was sent to take Jesus' place as our intercessor on the earth, Jesus is our high priest and intercessor in heaven, to quite God's wrath against us when we fail to do God's good pleasure or perfect will for our life to the fullest; of course this is true … only … if we are actively pursuing God's perfect will for our life, which we are commanded to do (Hebrews 6:1-2). As long as we are making the … Effort… to obey, go onto Perfection (sanctification of our physical body); Jesus' Atonement (Grace) will cover the inevitable failure to perfectly obey God as a result of the sinful nature that still remains in our physical body. The Bible teaches explicitly against abusing God's Grace to live as WE desire, if we do abuse, there "could be" eternal negative repercussions; being denied eternal life at Jesus' Judgment Seat (Matthew 7:21, Romans 8:1, 1 Corinthians 9:27, Galatians 5:13, 1 Peter 2:16; Revelation 3:1-5).

Not everyone that says unto me, Lord, Lord, shall enter into the kingdom of heaven; but he

that does the will of my Father which is in heaven. Matthew 7:21

But I keep under my body, and bring it into subjection: lest that by any means, when I have preached to others, I myself should be a castaway (Gr. rejected). 1 Corinthians 9:27

For, brethren, you have been called unto liberty; only use not liberty for an occasion to the flesh, but by love do service to one another. Galatians 5:13

As free, and not using your liberty for a cloak of maliciousness (Gr. wickedness and depravity), but as the servants of God. 1 Peter 2:16

I compare Parakletos (advocate) similar to what Moses did in behalf of the Children of Israel when God was so angry with them that He wanted to wipe them out and raise up children to Moses to take their place. Moses interceded for the Children of Israel, by letting God know that if He did that, He would dishonor Himself before the heathen, causing them to say, that He has brought them out into the desert only to kill them and thereby making Him Self out to be one who cannot be trusted to keep His promises. Moses' intercession was enough to quiet God's anger; but not against Judgment for their constant rebellion. The Comforter, Counselor, Advocate, Lawyer, Helper, the Holy Spirit defends and intercedes for those who are God's faithful and true Saints, His Sons and Daughters.

The Holy Spirit gives us Mighty Power to obey God's perfect will. Those who teach God's Spirit is an insentient "it" (only the power of God) purposely ignore or twist references that PROVE the Holy Spirit is a sentient "HE," they having made a CHOICE to remain deceived. The Holy Spirit is God's personal Spirit like we have one of our own (Matthew 10:20). Luke 1:35 lets us know the Holy Spirit USED the Power of the Highest (Almighty God), not insemination, to CREATE the body of Jesus in Mary's womb.

There is plenty of information in the Old Testament to support God's Spirit is a separate identity apart from Almighty God, having His own identity function and purpose; i.e. the Spirit of the Lord / the Spirit of God. God who is a Spirit has His own personal Spirit and soul like we have them (Leviticus 26:11-12). Since God is Deity His personal Spirit would be also; not to mean a separate "God" but equal in deity being God's personal Spirit. The Bible teaches a trinity (three) exist, Father Son and Holy

Spirit; how to define the THREE, their relevance, and relationship to each other is where the division in Theology lays.

For it is not you that speak but the ... Spirit OF your Father... which speaks in you Matthew 10:20

"But you shall receive power (Gr. Dunamis), after that the Holy Spirit is come upon you: and you shall be witnesses unto me both in Jerusalem, and in all Judaea, and in Samaria, and unto the uttermost part of the earth" Acts 1:8. The Greek word translated Power, DUNAMIS (doo'-nam-is) in Acts 1:8, refers to the Holy Spirit giving us not just power to be witnesses, but MIGHTY POWER, power to perform miracles, moral power and excellence of soul. The Holy Spirit is the one who gives us the power to obey God to the fullness of the degree that He requires, and to learn and understand what is God's perfect will for our life (1 Corinthians 2:16).

For who has known the mind of the Lord, that he may instruct (Gr. agree with) him? But we have the mind of Christ. 1 Corinthians 2:16

It can be claimed that Jesus is the first to receive the Baptism with the Holy Spirit, after John baptized

Him in water, when John saw God's Spirit descend and REMAIN on Jesus, and God could be heard calling Jesus His Son in whom I am well pleased (Matthew 3:13-17, John 1:33 and 8:29); this also proves three identities exist. After which God's Spirit led Jesus into the wilderness to be tempted by Satan. It was after the wilderness Victory that Jesus did His first recorded miracle, in Cana of Galilee, fulfilling another prophecy about Him. It was as a result of the Holy Spirit Baptism that Jesus' ministry and purpose from the very beginning having been BORN "Lord AND Savior" began (Luke 2:11, John 12:27). At least seven of the Gifts mentioned in 1 Corinthians 12:8-11 functioned through Jesus' life as recorded in the Gospels.

John 17:3 tells us, under the New Covenant we NOW need BOTH the Father and Son as our "Lord and Savior" to receive eternal life. Without Jesus as Lord and Savior, God who is Lord and Savior also will not grant the hope and promise of eternal life to anyone (John 14:6); except those who have never heard about Jesus and God's Plan of Salvation. According to Romans 2:11-16 God will Judge those who have never heard, for eternal life or not, based on whether they obeyed God's moral laws that He included with the creation of our spirit and soul (Genesis 1:26).

Then Jesus came from Galilee to Jordan unto John, to be baptized of him. But John forbad him, saying, I have need to be baptized of you, and come you to me? And Jesus answering said unto him, suffer it to be so now: for thus it becomes us to fulfill all righteousness. Then he suffered him. And Jesus, when he was baptized, went up straightway out of the water: and, lo, the heavens were opened unto him, and he saw the Spirit of God descending like a dove, and lighting upon him: And lo a voice from heaven, saying, This is my beloved Son, in whom I am well pleased. Mathew 3:13-17

And I knew him not: but he that sent me to baptize with water, the same said unto me, Upon whom you shall see the Spirit descending, and remaining on him, the same is he which baptizes with the Holy Spirit. John 1:33

For unto you is born this day in the city of David a Savior, which is Christ the Lord. Luke 2:11

Jesus taught us information about what the Baptism with the Holy Spirit would accomplish in and through OUR life, obviously as this Baptism did in and through His, as recorded in John chapters

14-16 (Jesus reminded the Apostles of this instruction in Acts 1:4), and after His resurrection instructed the Apostles to wait in Jerusalem until they received the same Baptism with the Holy Spirit (Luke 24:49, Acts 1:8). Jesus anointed (ordained) the Apostles for ministry when He breathed on them in John 20:21-23; that was neither the Baptism with the Holy Spirit that they were to receive on the Day of Pentecost nor was it the Baptism when He gave them the ability to understand the Scriptures that He taught them about Himself (Luke 24:44) as recorded in Luke 24:45 which v49 verifies. There are those who want to believe God's New Birth was also given on the Day of Pentecost; this could very well be true because of Jesus' comment to Peter "when you are converted" and Peter's statement in 1 Peter 1:3 that it is as a result of Jesus' resurrection we receive God's New Birth (anagenneo: begotten again).

And, being assembled together with them, commanded them that they should not depart from Jerusalem, but wait for the promise of the Father, which, said he, you have heard of me. Acts 1:4

And, behold, I send the promise of my Father upon you: but tarry you in the city of Jerusalem,

until you be endued with power from on high. Luke 24:49

But you shall receive power, after that the Holy Spirit is come upon you: and you shall be witnesses unto me both in Jerusalem, and in all Judaea, and in Samaria, and unto the uttermost part of the earth. Acts 1:8

Blessed be the God and Father of our Lord Jesus Christ, which according to his abundant mercy has begotten us again unto a lively hope by the resurrection of Jesus Christ from the dead, 1 Peter 1:3

As recorded in Hebrews 6:2 there is a doctrine of BAPTISMS, which validates … more … than one kind of baptism exists. The ONE Baptism spoken about in Ephesians 4:5, using CONTEXT, is referring only to God's New Birth (the baptism … IN … the Holy Spirit), not, that there is only one kind of baptism which Hebrew 6:2 supports. The most significant Baptism a person NEEDS to receive the promise and hope of eternal life is God's New Birth. God's New Birth MUST be received first, before water baptism has any relevance, and before God will Baptist anyone WITH His Holy Spirit.

In Act 10:44-48 God gave the Baptism with the Holy Spirit to Gentile believers ... before ... they were baptized in water, which is one more source reference that proves water baptism ... does not ... provide God's New Birth. A person MUST be born again FIRST before God will baptize anyone with the Holy Spirit, and like Jesus taught in John 3:3-6 God's Spirit is the one who accomplishes the New Birth in our spirit and soul. The New Testament Scriptures teach that THREE kinds of baptisms exist; The "baptism IN the Holy Spirit" which is the New Birth Jesus said we must receive to enter into and see (Gr. perceive, discern, and discover) the kingdom of God (John 3:3-6), "Water baptism" after receiving the New Birth, and the "Baptism WITH the Holy Spirit" with which we receive God's Power, Glossolalia, and the Nine Gifts (charismata). What is written in Acts 10:44-48 and Acts 19:2-6 lets us know God gave the Baptism with the Holy Spirit either before water baptism or after water baptism.

But this shall be the covenant that I will make with the house of Israel; After those days, says the Lord, I will put my law in their inward parts, and write it in their hearts; and will be their God, and they shall be my people. And they shall teach no more every man his neighbor, and every man his brother, saying, Know the Lord: for they shall

all know me, from the least of them unto the greatest of them, says the Lord: for I will forgive their iniquity, and I will remember their sin no more. Jeremiah 31:33-34

Then Peter said unto them, Repent, and be baptized every one of you in the name of Jesus Christ for the remission of sins, and ye shall receive the gift of the Holy Spirit. Acts 2:38

And suddenly there came a sound from heaven as of a rushing mighty wind, and it filled all the house where they were sitting. And there appeared unto them cloven tongues like as of fire, and it sat upon each of them. And they were all filled with the Holy Spirit, and began to speak with other tongues, as the Spirit gave them utterance. Acts 2:2-4

And from Jesus Christ, who is the faithful witness, and the first begotten of the dead, and the prince of the kings of the earth. Unto him that loved us, and washed us from our sins in his own blood, Revelation 1:5

And they sung a new song, saying, You are worthy to take the book, and to open the seals thereof: for you were slain, and have redeemed us

to God with your blood out of every kindred, and tongue, and people, and nation; Revelation 5:9

I received the Baptism with the Holy Spirit when I asked for this Baptism … after … I received Jesus as Lord and Savior of my life while alone in my Apartment July 8 1972, six weeks prior to my nineteenth birthday. God gave me a few words in my mind to speak, but I have heard the Glossolalia flow out of the mouth of others with no forethought; God is not restricted to one way to Baptized with His Spirit, as the Book of Acts validates. The common practice by the Apostles is that they laid their hands on the believer to receive God's Baptism with Holy Spirit. As a result of how God gave me the Baptism, when I pray for a Christian to receive this God given Baptism, I pray God will give them a few words in their mind so they can speak them … IF … they do not begin to speak without any "forethought."

It is NOT Biblical to "couch" a person what to speak, that is GOD'S Responsibility not ours. God's Baptism was given to Israeli believers first (Acts 2:2-4) and to Gentiles believers second (Acts 10:44-46). Conversion (the New Birth), Water baptism, and the Baptism with the Holy Spirit are THREE different and distinct Baptisms. Jeremiah 31:31-34 clearly validates Israelis were to receive God's New

Birth and the Baptism with the Holy Spirit before the Gentiles; therefore Acts 2 and 10 is the evidence Jeremiah 31:31-34 was fulfilled this way.

For a person to conclude the "Baptism WITH the Holy Spirit" is ...not... a ONE TIME event in our life is a false conclusion. There is no evidence this Baptism existed under the Old Covenant; for Jeremiah 31:33-34 validates "God's New Birth" and the "Baptism WITH the Holy Spirit" are SOLELY Two New Covenant Events, and it is these TWO EVENTS that unequivocally prove to the recipient that the Bible is the Word of God and anything to the contrary is a Lie and Deception of Satan. Multiple times of anointing were common under the Old Covenant, and no less under the New Covenant, Acts 4:8 is one example; therefore the Baptism with the Holy Spirit is ... not ... the same event as the "multiple times of anointing" for ministry.

God's "multiple times of anointing" is not controlled by us but BY HIM, like the Nine Gifts [charismata] of the Holy Spirit are controlled by Him as recorded in 1 Corinthians 12:11. Under the Mosaic (Old) Covenant God's Spirit would descend on people but never permanently dwell in them 24/7 like He does now under the New Covenant through the Baptism with the Holy Spirit. A minister can be ANOINTED multiple times by the Holy Spirit for ministry without having God's Baptism with the Holy Spirit; the Baptism that gives us God's Power, Glossolalia, and the Nine Charismata (Gifts), which defines and distinguishes this Baptism from the anointing to preach and God's New Birth Event.

But all these work that one and the selfsame Spirit, dividing to every man severally as He will. 1 Corinthians 12:11

Based on Paul's teaching there are "tongues" that MY spirit speaks and those which GOD's Spirit speaks through those who have the Baptism WITH the Holy Spirit. The "tongues" (glossolalia) God has given MY spirit the ability to speak are spoken by me to Him not to anyone around me, but Paul cautions that when we do worship and pray in "tongues" that we alternate with our birth language also so that those around us can be edified or benefited by our worship and prayer. God knows what I am saying to HIM; therefore no interpretation is needed.

The "Gift of Tongues" that GOD Speaks ...through... me is a message from HIM to someone else or the whole congregation; it is this Function BY God that Requires the "Gift of Interpretation" so that those who hear what was said can understand with their birth language what God is saying. This explains why Paul said if any speak in an unknown tongue PRAY that you may interpret, he was referring to the Gift of Tongues and Gift of Interpretation that GOD Speaks through us. Obviously if there is no one who God can anoint to Interpret, we need to be the one He will use to do this.

A person would be in ...error... to claim the Baptism with the Holy Spirit that happened on the Day of Pentecost was only for the Apostles, since 120 were in the Upper Room and all who were present received this Baptism, which included Mary and her other children. The Day of Pentecost was the first recorded incident in the Book of Acts when "Tongues" were a manifestation of the Baptism with the Holy Spirit in the form of xenolalia (earthly languages); glossolalia is (angelic languages). There are five recorded occasions when Christians received the Baptism with the Holy Spirit in the Book of Acts, which doctrine can be created from. I have heard a minister, who taught against the Baptism, teach "tongues are ONLY languages of the earth," totally ignoring what Paul wrote in 1 Corinthians 13:1 "though I speak with the tongues of MEN and of ANGELS." Tongues ...are not...only languages of the earth, and calling them gibberish is sacrilegious, and would likely be blasphemy against the Holy Spirit.

Though I speak with the tongues of men and of angels, and have not charity, I am become as sounding brass, or a tinkling cymbal. 1 Corinthians 13:1

If a person goes looking for reasons to reproach (blaspheme) the Baptism with the Holy Spirit today, Satan is more than willing to oblige them. There was a Blasphemer who wrote an article about his investigation into demonic forms of worship and practices in which he wrote he heard them speak in tongues; he used this observation to … ignorantly … conclude that Speaking in Tongues is demonic and of the Devil. The blindness of Satan on preachers like this one is insidious.

Since Demons are Fallen "angels," and there are "tongues of angels," it should be obvious that Demons have languages just like Holy Angels do. There are earthly languages and there are angelic languages, which 1 Corinthians 13:1 validates. What the Blasphemer heard were DEMONS speaking through those demon possessed Pagans. Demonic manifestations do not invalidate GOD's TRUE manifestations still exist today; a person is deceived to believe otherwise. Based on how Jesus defined Blasphemy against the Holy Spirit it is to SPEAK against what the Holy Spirit does as having the origin with a Demon (Matthew 12:24-32, Mark 3:22-30).

And the scribes who came down from Jerusalem said, He has Beelzebub, and by the prince of the devils casts he out devils. And he called them unto him, and said unto them in parables, How can Satan cast out Satan? And if a kingdom be divided against itself, that kingdom cannot stand. And if a house be divided against itself, that house cannot stand. And if Satan rise up against himself, and be divided, he cannot stand, but has an end. No man can enter into a strong man's house, and spoil his goods, except he will first bind the strong man; and then he will spoil his house. Verily I say unto you, All sins shall be forgiven unto the sons of men, and blasphemies where with so ever they shall blaspheme: But he that shall blaspheme against the Holy Spirit hath never forgiveness, but is in danger of eternal damnation. Because they said, He has an unclean spirit. Mark 3:22-30

Paul quoted, as a DUAL prophecy Isaiah 28:11, in 1 Corinthians 14:21-22 that the glossolalia is the sign (confirmation) for the unconverted (those who believe not). Paul's meaning is, for those who do not believe

God exists and/or that do not believe the Gospel is true and that Jesus is God's promised Messiah. The reason I wrote "dual prophesy," a common practice by the Apostles, such as Isaiah 7:14, is because if you read the Context for Isaiah 28:11 it is about Israel going into Captivity, their enemies "mocking" them in a language they did not understand; the verse has nothing to do with the glossolalia, but it does as a proof text for God's Existence and that Jesus IS God's Promised Messiah.

I will not go into the significant reason for each of the nine charismata (Gifts). What I want to share is the BENEFIT God gives with the Glossolalia, which many believe is the "initial evidence" the "First Manifested Proof," as recorded in the Book of Acts for three of the five occasions WHEN a Christian received the Baptism with the Holy Spirit, and a fourth of the five times that can be proven with Paul's confession about himself in 1 Corinthians 14:18. On four of the five occasions when Christians received the Baptism with the Holy Spirit in the Book of Acts; it can be proven that the Glossolalia was spoken, with prophesying included for one of the four. It is only on one of the five occasions that Luke records nothing about any manifestation, but is generally accepted that the Glossolalia was the manifested proof for everyone to know a Christian had received the Baptism with the Holy Spirit, since there are four times that can prove the Glossolalia was the manifested proof. The scripture references are Acts 2:4, Acts 8:17, Acts 9:17, Acts 10:44-46, and Acts 19:6.

And they were all filled with the Holy Spirit, and began to speak with other tongues, as the Spirit gave them utterance. Acts 2:4

Then laid they their hands on them, and they received the Holy Spirit. Acts 8:17

And Ananias went his way, and entered into the house; and putting his hands on him said, Brother Saul, the Lord, even Jesus, that appeared unto you in the way as you came, has sent me, that you might receive your sight, and be filled with the Holy Spirit. Acts 9:17 (1 Cor. 14:18)

While Peter yet spoke these words, the Holy Spirit fell on all them which heard the word. And they of the circumcision which believed were astonished, as many as came with Peter, because that on the Gentiles also was poured out the gift of the Holy Spirit. For they heard them speak with tongues, and magnify God... Acts 10:44-46

And when Paul had laid his hands upon them, the Holy Spirit came on them; and they spoke with tongues, and prophesied. Acts 19:6

A definition for the Greek word "oikodomeo" translated "edify" in 1 Corinthians 14:4a is as follows: "to edify or to build; to promote growth in Christian wisdom, affection, grace, virtue, holiness; blessedness to grow in wisdom and piety. Jude in Jude 1:20 tells us "But you, beloved, building up (epoikodomeo) yourselves on your most holy faith, praying in the Holy Spirit." God has provided for all of us a massive benefit and provision to accelerate the manifestation of God's righteousness and Resident Power through our life by His Baptism WITH the Holy Spirit and glossolalia to pray to and worship Him (1 Corinthians 14:14-18), and why Paul wrote that he spoke in the glossolalia more than the Corinthian Christians did; Paul knew the accelerated potential and spiritual benefits associated with doing this.

For if I pray in an unknown tongue (xenolalia or glossolalia), my spirit prays, but my understanding is unfruitful. What is it then? I will pray with the spirit, and I will pray with the understanding also: I will sing with the spirit, and I will sing with the understanding also. Else when you shall bless with the spirit, how shall he that occupies the room of

the unlearned say Amen at thy giving of thanks, seeing he understands not what you are saying? For you verily give thanks well, but the other is not edified. I thank my God, I speak with tongues more than you all: 1 Corinthians 14:14-18

Satan knows the Baptism with the Holy Spirit makes us more than conquerors against the sinful nature in our physical body, and a greater threat against his wicked destructive devises and agenda in the world. It is for this reason, if he can prevent anyone from receiving the Baptism with the Holy Spirit, through fear, intimidation, and doctrinal lies and deceptions, he has accomplished his goal; to keep us powerless and woefully defeated adversaries against him, and the demonic powers of darkness associated with his doomed kingdom. Do you want to stay weak and woefully defeated and oppressed or be more than a conqueror?

The answer should be "more than a conqueror." Ask God to fill you with the Baptism that HE has ALWAYS intended for us to receive after we have been born again by His Spirit through Jesus as Lord and Savior of our life. Paul wrote in 1 Corinthians 1:5-8 "That in EVERYTHING you are ENRICHED by Him, in all utterance, and in all knowledge; Even as the testimony of Christ was confirmed in you:

So that you come behind in no gift; waiting for the coming of our Lord Jesus Christ: Who shall confirm you unto the end, that you may be blameless in the day of our Lord Jesus Christ."

In 2009 the Lord gave me a sermon to preach to a congregation in Hollister Ohio titled "Revival Status;" here is what He gave me for the concluding remarks (edited for better clarity):

Sometime between 1909 and 1911 William P. Merrill wrote "Rise Up O Men of God," at the time Pastor of the Brick Presbyterian Church in New York NY [during the years of the Billy Sunday Revivalist campaigns, who himself was a licensed Presbyterian Minister], this was also the period when receiving the Holy Spirit with the Glossolalia was creating a time of revival throughout the world, William wrote:

Rise up O men of God! Have done with lesser things, give heart and mind and soul and strength to serve the King of Kings.

Rise up, O men of God! His kingdom tarries long; bring in the brotherhood and end the night of wrong.

Rise up, O men of God! The church for you doth wait. Her strength unequal to her task; rise up, and make her great!

Lift high the cross of Christ! Tread where His feet have trod; as brothers of the Son of man, rise up, O men of God!

Rise up O child of God refuse to wallow in the pig pin of spiritual weakness, and become a force against the Enemy to be reckoned with! The Enemy knows a Christian Baptized WITH the Holy Spirit is a significant threat to him, and his wicked agenda and devices. Living a fully obedient life before God is a maturing process that takes the endowment of God's power, which accompanies the Baptism with the Holy Spirit, God's 24/7 anointing upon our lives, to be able to do His perfect will for our life.

The Holy Spirit gives us the ability to hear God speak, and the endowment of power gives us the ability to do what He says. Without the Baptism with Holy Spirit we can never live the FULNESS of the Standard of Holiness that God requires of us, nor can we know and discern what is happening on God's divine level, what is about to happen in the near future, in the earth. A consecrated life of total obedience to God, and separation from all worldliness and its "religious" spirit full of carnal stench, coupled with the Power of the Holy Spirit, makes it possible for us to pillage ruthlessly the kingdom of darkness, and take territory for Christ; the salvation of souls.

Ask God to fill you with the Baptism WITH the Holy Spirit that HE has ALWAYS intended for us to receive after we have been Born Again by His Spirit through Jesus as Lord and Savior of our life.

Be encouraged always and go deep in your walk with God not shallow.

SOURCES

Biblical quotes are from the King James Version of the Bible, unless otherwise indicated, and edited with modern English.

Rise up o men of God written by William P. Merrill

Strong's Lexicon for Greek word definitions

The articles that provided the historical information over the centuries that document those who reported their account of the Baptism with the Holy Spirit comes from these Websites:

http://web.newworldencyclopedia.org/entry/Glossolalia

https://www.revolvy.com/main/index.php?s=Gustav%20 von%20Below

http://enrichmentjournal.ag.org/200602/200602_142_ Legacies.cfm

ABOUT THE AUTHOR

 I was born August 20, 1953 to Clara Ann Spencer and Samuel Andrew Siders in Columbus Ohio. Through a series of life events by the age of fifteen the Lord made His love for me real in my heart telling me that someday I would give my heart to Him. For three and a half years the Holy Spirit did the work of bringing me to the Radical Life Changing Born Again Event that Jeremiah defined in Jeremiah 31:33-34, Ezekiel in Ezekiel 36:26, Jesus in John 3:3-6 and Apostle Paul in 2 Corinthians 5:17. July 8, 1972 six weeks before my nineteenth birthday I was radically Born Again by God's Spirit and received God's Baptism WITH the Holy Spirit after being Born Again. July 8 1972 was on a Saturday; in the evening of Sunday July 9 1972 I was baptized in water.

July 2004 the Lord called me to preach, and led me to enroll in the Appalachian District School of Ministry (ADSOM) through the Assemblies of God in Ghent West Virginia. The Lord has been using me as an Apologist for over ten years to defend the Scriptures through Biblical Systematic Doctrine and Theology, and with Historical and Cuneiform Archaeological proofs. As a result He has given me a seminary level education through research and experience to be an effective Apologist for … HIM … to be glorified through my life. As is written in Jude 1:3 "Beloved, when I gave all diligence to write unto you of the common salvation, it was needful for me to write unto you, and exhort you that you should … earnestly contend … for the faith which was once delivered unto the saints;" therefore at this time in my life God is using me to fulfill this Ministry.

Other Books published by Samuel Siders

God requires far more of us than most Believers
are willing to live. Refusing to comply could
mean being rejected at the Judgement.

E-mail address to correspond with the author:
samuside@aol.com

Domain name for direct access to order more books:
www.thesevenchurchesofasia.com

To order books by phone, call toll free: 1-888-280-7715

AuthorHouse web address to self-publish your book:
www.authorhouse.com

Printed in the United States
By Bookmasters